From Tragedy to Triumph

Jeremiah Klaas

TRILOGY CHRISTIAN PUBLISHERS

TUSTIN, CA

Trilogy Christian Publishers

A Wholly Owned Subsidary of Trinity Broadcasting Network

2442 Michelle Drive

Tustin, CA 92780

For information, address Trilogy Christian Publishing

Rights Department, 2442 Michelle Drive, Tustin, Ca 92780.

Trilogy Christian Publishing/ TBN and colophon are trademarks of Trinity Broadcasting Network.

For information about special discounts for bulk purchases, please contact Trilogy Christian Publishing.

Manufactured in the United States of America

10 9 8 7 6 5 4 3 2 1

Library of Congress Cataloging-in-Publication Data is available.

ISBN 978-1-64773-064-2

ISBN 978-1-64773-065-9

Contents

*This book is dedicated to those struggling with addictions,
mental illness, and living in a hopeless situation.*

God loves you and wants you healed and set free.

Acknowledgements

Thank you to all who contributed to my journey from tragedy to triumph.

Special thanks to Donna Jones and Steven Lilgreen in helping me put my story on paper and made this book a reality.

Introduction

Life is a journey, and at times, it is good to look back in order to see how far we've come. This book is a testimony to the glory of God and how He rescued me from dark days and then equipped me to teach and preach the love of God. My journey began as a mischievous boy who fell in with the wrong crowd. I was involved with drugs and alcohol, I got in trouble with the law, and ultimately, the doctors diagnosed me with an incurable disease.

My emotional and physical healing didn't happen instantly but was a process that took many years to understand. I share my healing testimony to help others understand that God loves them, and because of this, He wouldn't make healing hard or impossible to achieve. I, on the other hand, found it difficult to receive healing, especially when I started to learn about God's desire and ability to heal.

Throughout my journey, I saw healings through my hands, yet I was still living with symptoms. I couldn't understand why I didn't see healing in my body, and it appeared to be a long, drawn-out process. I got frustrated and wanted to give up. I read healing Scriptures every day and had given God my whole heart, even quoting God's Word. However, something wasn't connecting when it came to my healing. I have learned that there were some things in my life that were blocking my ability to receive the manifestation of my healing.

God doesn't want anyone to struggle to receive healing. My goal is to share the things that blocked my ability to receive healing in the hope, it will help others. Removing blockages will enable others to walk in victory in all areas of their lives. I received complete healing from Multiple Sclerosis, drugs, alcohol, and mental and physical issues. My heart is to share how all these issues were healed through understanding and standing on the truth of the Word of God.

He sent His word and healed them, And delivered them from their destructions.
(Psalm 107:20 NKJV)

These truths set me free from everything that was wrong in my life. My testimony is to the power of God and how I had to lay down my life in order to find it. I found true victory in Christ when I finally allowed God to live inside of me by the power of the Holy Spirit and having that relationship with God.

Through my journey, I found the only way was through a personal relationship with Jesus Christ and His Word. I pray my testimony glorifies God and helps others see that there is a way to get out of their problems and restore their lives.

Early Years

My life began in a small town in Ohio. I would like to say I was a normal boy growing up, playing baseball, and going to county fairs, but in truth, I was a troubled child who started messing around with alcohol at a young age. Church, faith, and religion were not a part of my life. When I look back, I see how God carried me through all these years as a child, even though I didn't know who He was. That is how good God is.

I wasn't very good at school and had a hard time focusing on reading as well as completing my homework assignments. The bottom line is that I had a hard time with just about everything in my youth. To help get a sense of what I mean about my troubled past, here are a couple of incidents that stick out in my memory.

I didn't make it easy on my fourth-grade teacher, and she had a difficult time dealing with me. One day, she decided to put my desk next to hers in order to keep an eye on me. I guess she figured sitting me right out in the open might cause me to behave. Unfortunately, that didn't seem to help the situation because I continued to bother her and now even distracted her while she was teaching the other students. Her next step was to move me to the back of the room, facing the wall. This made things worse, and she ultimately removed me entirely from her classroom by moving me and my desk and setting it outside the classroom in the hallway. While this final act helped the teacher and the rest of the students, it pushed me further away from learning and into more trouble down the road.

Another incident where I caused havoc for my teacher was jumping out the window when I felt like playing instead of learning. While in the classroom looking out the window and seeing a beautiful sunny day, my desire was to be playing outside rather than learning about math, science, and history. Playing and running around outside was more desirable to me. I decided that the swings looked very appealing, and I would jump out the window when my teacher's back was turned. My classmates laughed but my teacher didn't think it was funny. She had to come outside and drag me back into the classroom. My only thought was to have fun, and for me, school wasn't any fun and I didn't feel I needed to be there. I know this was disruptive and had a lasting effect on my teacher and classmates. However, all I wanted to do was have fun.

I don't know why, but while I sat in a classroom, my mind would race 100 miles an hour. I couldn't focus on schoolwork or anything, and all I wanted to do was be outside. These are only two of a long list of incidents that occurred during my school years to show that I was out of control.

During my school days (when I wasn't jumping out windows to play), I would daydream about being on my uncle's dairy farm. Working on my uncle's farm is the happy memory that I cherish. What boy doesn't like getting on a tractor and driving it even before having his driver's license? I loved working with my hands and taking care of all the animals. I especially loved doing my daily chores because it kept me from getting in trouble. I spent most of my youth, from about age nine to eighteen, working at this farm. Any free moment I had was spent there. I didn't want to be anywhere else.

I was full of energy and had a hard time sitting still. Being in the classroom was difficult and seemed to drive me toward getting into trouble at school. I experimented with alcohol when I was in junior high school. Once I started drinking, things got worse, and I was headed down a dark path. The alcohol affected my brain and enabled bad thoughts to creep in and caused me to get into even more trouble in high school.

One day the superintendent called me into his office and asked me, "Do you want to be here in school?" My reply was "No". Then he said, "Why don't you just quit?" And I said, "That is a great idea." He handed me some papers that I signed, and then I left the building—Never to look back.

When I quit school, I continued drinking and that ruined everything, including my relationships. I was full of energy and didn't know how to harness it. I don't know why, but I liked getting into trouble. It is hard to believe that God would eventually use me to minister to and help others.

This is just a quick glimpse of the early years of my life. It wasn't all bad. As I mentioned, I do have some great memories growing up and working on my uncle's farm. I also had lots of friends. My intent in sharing about my past is not to blame anyone—it is to provide a snapshot of the person I was and show how God turned a troubled life like mine into a victorious life and to help others see there is a way out.

CHAPTER 2

Wrong Crowd

Here I was, an alcoholic high school dropout who loved to get into trouble. This was not a good situation. Since I wasn't in school or working, I had a lot of free time on my hands. I started hanging out with some of my dad's friends. I don't think my dad knew that they were involved with drugs, and neither did I until this world of drugs was exposed to me.

I went from casual drinking and taking drugs with friends to hanging out in bars full time. The drugs fueled my mischievous behavior to getting involved in doing bad things such as four DUIs (Driving Under the Influence), resisting arrest, and disorderly conduct for striking a cop. I hardly worked, and when I did, I wasn't productive. This crazy lifestyle led me to be arrested at least a dozen times.

One time, the chief of police, along with another officer, came into a bar where I was causing a ruckus. I felt someone touch my shoulder, I turned around swinging, and ended up striking one of the officers. I didn't mean to hit him—it was a reaction to the touch on my shoulder. I was sorry, but unfortunately for me, I had already hit him. I was arrested and thrown into jail. The cops seemed to like me as I typically didn't stay long in jail, and someone always bailed me out.

When I wasn't in jail, I was helping a friend remodel homes. Many times, after spending the night partying with friends in the local bars, not sleeping or if so, only a couple of hours, I would then set off to work at a construction site. At those times, breakfast would consist of drugs to get me started even though I was already high and drunk from the previous night since I never really sobered up.

Only by God's grace did I not kill myself as I climbed ladders and used power tools. One day I fell off a ladder about twenty feet high. My head landed on a pipe that was sticking up out of the ground. I'm sure the alcohol and drugs helped to mask the pain I might have experienced as I never even went to the hospital or to see a doctor. As I got up off the ground, my jaw was stuck. Instead of heading to the hospital, I decided it was better to go to the bar to take away any pain. My jaw would eventually reset itself as I continued to party; barely sleeping, eating, and remodeling homes.

I didn't know God at this time in my life, but God had healed me so many times as I did dumb things. Like cutting off a cast with a pair of pliers when I twisted and broke my ankle after stepping in a hole. I rode my Harley home and went to a doctor's office the next day after my leg swelled up. He put a cast on my leg and told me not to walk on it for about six weeks. After two and a half weeks, I had had enough of the cast and tore it off with a pair of pliers. Of course, alcohol and drugs enabled me to function during this time, as well as so many other crazy times.

I was complete entertainment for the town and folks in the bars. No one had any idea what I would do next from walking on top of a bar to stealing a motorcycle right from under the owner's nose. The crazier I got, the more entertaining I became. To this day, I'm not allowed in some of the bars back home, not that I would want to be there.

Another drug/alcohol-related situation happened when a guy put a gun to my head during a drug deal. I was so messed up that I thought it would be a relief if the guy pulled the trigger. I told him to do me a favor, pull the trigger, and end this messed up, crazy life I was living. Praise God, he didn't pull the trigger, but regretfully, he ended up giving me the drugs I wanted and didn't even charge me.

This paints a picture of where I was mentally. I thought dying was the only escape out of the lifestyle I had created. My life had spiraled out of control through bad choices, drugs, and alcohol. However, God had other plans for me, but first, my life would spiral even more out of control.

CHAPTER 3

Bad Diagnosis

I've learned that a Holy God took my mess and gave me a message. My goal for sharing my trials is not to glorify my mess. It is to show the transforming power of God through Jesus Christ and what He can do for a person so broken and hurt.

While still involved with drugs and alcohol, I met a woman who was involved in the same lifestyle. I thought having somebody in my life would help me, but our relationship was not a healthy one, and we ended up getting into trouble together. We met in the drug world, which wasn't too smart and caused a lot of trouble. We would eventually part ways.

One day as I walked down the street, the left side of my body went completely numb. I thought I was having a stroke from all the cocaine I was doing. I immediately went to the doctor's office. The doctor relieved my fear of a stroke but sent me to a specialist to confirm his suspicion of a life-altering diagnosis of Multiple Sclerosis (MS). After a series of magnetic resonance imaging

(MRI) and a spinal tap, I was told I had MS, an incurable disease.

"MS is a long-lasting disease that can affect your brain, spinal cord, and the optic nerves in your eyes. It can cause problems with vision, balance, muscle control, and other basic body functions. The effects are often different for everyone" ("Multiple Sclerosis: What Is MS? Overview, Risk Factors and Outlook" 2019). "The disease causes damage resulting in your brain not sending signals through your body correctly" ("Multiple Sclerosis: What Is MS? Overview, Risk Factors and Outlook" 2019). "Your nerves also don't work as they should to help you move and feel" ("Multiple Sclerosis: What Is MS? Overview, Risk Factors and Outlook" 2019).

My initial reaction was, "like, whatever," and I continued in my normal routine of buying alcohol and drugs. I think I really hit rock bottom when I received the MS diagnosis on top of an already drug and alcohol problem. I didn't know what to do but believed I needed to get sober with no idea about how to achieve it. As the diagnosis started to settle in my mind, I began to realize, "I'm sick, I don't feel good, and I have no hope."

My spirit was crushed, but I was able to muster up the strength to find help. Maybe deep down inside of me, there was the will to live. I knew I needed to try something because what I had been doing with my life so far wasn't working. The drugs and alcohol that I thought helped my life in the past were making me feel worse due to the MS. The sickness was now taking over my mind and body.

I stopped taking drugs and alcohol on my own and tried to live a clean life. I didn't have Jesus in my life, so I was doing this with my own strength. I did good for a little while but then relapsed. For about two years, this cycle continued: get clean, relapse, get clean, relapse.

This roller coaster of a life was exhausting, and I couldn't take it anymore. I had bills piling up, a house I couldn't manage, and a job I physically couldn't do because of my limitations with MS. I just couldn't take it anymore and didn't see a way out. The only thing I knew was drugs and alcohol. I was at my last straw when I finally said, "I'm done. Enough is enough. I'm gonna end this messed up life." So, I decided to overdose using drugs and alcohol.

One crazy day, I started out drinking in a bar and then picked up some drugs. When the bar closed, I headed to a friend's house in order to take more drugs. Drugs make you paranoid, and I was already messed up because of the sickness, alcohol, and stress in my life, so things intensified. I suddenly had an urge to get out of town, so I left my friend's house and started walking. I said, "I'm just gonna walk."

As I started walking out of town, it was cold and snowing, and all I had on was a long-sleeve shirt. I knew I had to go about seven miles to my destination, and then I remembered I had some pills (Ativan) in my pocket. These pills were the equivalent of valium and I knew I had about twenty of them. I reached into my pocket and pulled out about eight of them and took them all at once figuring I would pass out and die on the side of the road. That is the place I was at mentally—it was a very dark place.

I put the rest of the pills back in the bottle and in my pocket. As I continued walking, I started to feel out of it. I was like, "Crap, I am gonna just take the rest of the pills to get this over with." I reached into my pocket, to pull out the bottle, and realized the rest of the pills were gone. To this day, I'm not sure what happened, but I believe God caused those pills to disappear somehow.

A drug addict is fully aware of the number of pills he or she has and where they are located. I know how cautious and aware I was when I took the eight pills out of the bottle, and I am positive I put the rest of them back in the bottle and into my pocket. I am sure I didn't drop the pills along the way. I was totally alert because that is what cocaine does to you, so I knew what I was doing at the time I put the bottle with the remaining pills back in my pocket. I felt safe knowing I had the drugs in my pocket because I could feel the bottle in my pants pocket. I personally think there was a supernatural encounter with God saving and sparing my life that night.

When I had reached into my pocket only to discover the pills were gone from the bottle, I thought the eight pills I had taken were causing me to lose my mind. Suddenly, I felt this amazing strength surging through my body. Almost like it was overpowering me and enabling me to finish the seven-mile walk. When I got to my destination, I collapsed on the floor and woke up the next morning, urinating blood because of the pills I had taken. I think I was in shock to discover I was alive. You would think this experience would cause me to change my ways, but no, I got a ride back to the bar I had left the previous day. I continued to drink, get more cocaine, and then locked myself alone in a building where I had permission to stay. I figured I would lock myself in and take enough drugs to end my life.

As the sun rose that next day, and I was still alive but a total wreck. I thought, "I cannot walk out of this place without help because I cannot do this anymore. I'm still alive, and I cannot shoot myself." I called a friend to come and get me, and he took me to the local hospital, where they transferred me to the psych ward. In the psych ward, the guy in the next bed told me about a place called *The Salvation Army.*

He said, "I've been to it before, and it's awesome. And it's free too." I responded, "That's perfect cuz I don't have any money."

I called for the nurse and shared what this man had told me about *The Salvation Army*. She called a cab for me, and I left the hospital heading for *The Salvation Army* in Akron, Ohio.

CHAPTER 4

Hey, You Got It!

When I arrived at *The Salvation Army*, I realized I didn't know anybody and felt totally lost, but I knew I needed to be there to get sober. As I went about my days getting sober, it seemed like everyone around me was talking about Jesus. Part of *The Salvation Army's* program is getting someone back on their feet and into a normal lifestyle. I was put in charge of the electronics where you test them for resale. The good ones were sold, and the bad ones were thrown away. I had a trainer in this program that showed me what to do. When he was released from the program, he happened to leave behind a Christian CD. Since I was testing electronics, there was a radio available for me to use. I had no desire to listen to Christian stuff as I was not there to find or follow Jesus. All I wanted out of this program was to get sober and go to motorcycle school in Florida.

For some reason, I put that CD into the CD player, and within seconds, a peace and the overwhelming presence of joy and love engulfed my entire body. I started singing out loud to the song playing on the CD. The people in the warehouse stopped what they were doing and stared at me. One of the guys across from my station yelled out, "I'm gonna follow you!" I didn't know what he meant at the time, but I knew enough to say, "Don't follow me." See, I knew I was a mess and didn't want anyone following in my footsteps. Someone left the warehouse to find the captain of *The Salvation Army* as it must have been a strange experience for the other workers. As the captain approached me, I felt he was studying me to understand what happened. I'm not sure I knew what was happening either, but I can tell you that the fear I had lived with was completely gone.

The captain said, "Hey, you got it." I asked, "I got what?" He replied, "You got Jesus!" My response to him was, "Oh, okay, well, whatever I got, it feels good, so great!" I had no clue what any of this meant but I know now that I received Jesus that day. I don't know if I had received Jesus when I was a child, but I can tell you at that moment, I had this peace and joy that is indescribable, and it stayed with me for the rest of the day.

The mixed-up ideas about giving up or quitting were no longer plaguing and consuming my thoughts. Even the nagging thoughts about my incurable disease disappeared at that moment. All the pressures that had built up in my life—sickness, drug and alcohol addiction—were now gone. That night, I slept all night for the first time in a very long time.

The next morning, I attended the mandatory chapel service. For some reason, I felt drawn to the front and knelt at the altar. I wasn't familiar with kneeling at the altar, but it seemed to come naturally today. I had a feeling I was supposed to be there at that altar. As I knelt, the same feeling I had the day before in the warehouse intensified to almost ten times, and I started weeping.

I think that was the first time I ever cried. I'm sure I must have cried sometime in my youth and past, but this felt like the first time. I think I cried for about fifteen minutes, and then I stood up and all these words were coming out and I was speaking about God. I don't even know what I said or what it meant, and it appeared the captain and his wife were unsure about what to do next. They asked those in attendance to leave and turned their full attention to me. They knew something powerful was happening with me and God and their next step was to call the general of *The Salvation Army*.

I went about my normal day in the warehouse, but something was different this time. I started to share words of encouragement with my co-workers, and I knew things that people around me needed to hear. It freaked them out, so the captain of *The Salvation Army* decided it would be better if I left. It must have thrown everyone for a loop because one day, I was not interested in Jesus, and the next day, I was completely on fire for Him.

Even though I was on fire for Jesus, I still knew nothing about Him or the Bible. The folks at *The Salvation Army* had never seen anyone have an instant conversion and something as radical as what I had experienced. It freaked them out, and they had to let me go. Unfortunately, I was released back into my old way of life. That was not a good life to go back to since I didn't have a commitment to God, never read the Bible, and I didn't know Jesus or fully understand what I had experienced. All I knew was I had a peace that I couldn't explain, and God had something to do with it.

I was on my own again and hanging with my old friends. They wanted me to drink and resume the life I had left. At first, I felt it wouldn't be a good idea for me to drink again, but the temptation was too great. My friend said, "Well, even Jesus drank wine." Since I didn't know the Scriptures, I thought, *Well, maybe that is true because I did know that Jesus turned water into wine.* This thought led me to have one drink with my friend, and the next thing I knew, I was back at the bar talking to people about Jesus and drinking at the same time. The people at the bar always thought I was a little crazy because of the drugs and alcohol, but now they thought

I was even crazier because all I could talk about was Jesus. I had such limited knowledge about Him, so all I could share was about His love and the experience I had at *The Salvation Army*.

Each time I shared, God would show up in amazing ways. He would reveal things to me about the people I met—things to help and encourage the people God put in my path. I felt so confused because I really didn't know what was happening. I felt God drawing me closer and closer to Him while, at the same time, using me to help others. I would continue to share Jesus the best way I knew how, which wasn't the greatest; however, I was obedient, and God guided and helped me every time.

CHAPTER 5

Hard Road to Recovery

After leaving *The Salvation Army*, I was living in my old neighborhood, back in my old lifestyle, sharing Jesus and drinking even more than before. I was so addicted to the alcohol that I had to start my morning with a drink. I couldn't eat breakfast without having a drink first. I knew I had a drug and alcohol problem before getting saved and born-again at *The Salvation Army*, but now the addiction was much worse. This addiction was robbing me of everything, even though I was sharing Jesus with everyone I met. I was a complete mess—a total disaster. I understand now that the devil was coming after me with everything he had because of my lack of understanding of God's Word and not being fully committed to Jesus. I was very vulnerable.

Because of my experience with God at *The Salvation Army*, I was operating under the power of God and the Holy Spirit, who was now living in me. I didn't know the

Word of God, I couldn't fight the addiction and temptations around me, and it felt like the enemy was out to destroy me. The enemy would have won, except God had a plan for my life.

I was in and out of rehab programs at least five times. Each time I would enter totally drunk and a disaster and never leave completely sober. In my lifetime, there was a total of five rehab programs because of the drugs and alcohol and two nursing home experiences due to the MS. None of these programs or experiences filled the void and hole in my heart—that could only be completely healed by Jesus Christ.

About two years after my encounter with Jesus at The Salvation Army, I decided to lock myself in a room with God—just Him and me. I prayed for hours and hours each day. There wasn't anything else I could do but pray. Quite a few times I realized it was two or three in the morning. During those times, I didn't want to stop praying because I felt bad thoughts would creep back into my mind. I was at the end of myself and asked God, "Where do you want me to go?" I heard God say, "Colorado Springs." This is where my story gets amazing and where I began getting the victory in my life. I said, "Yes" to God.

I knew I had enough money for a bus ticket to Colorado Springs, but I had to trust God for the rest. Where would I stay? How would I afford to live? Would God guide my steps? And would I learn to walk by faith?

I was sober, and I knew that I couldn't touch even one drink or do any drugs, and I was trusting in the Lord to help me stay clean. As I got off the bus in Colorado Springs, I began to share about Jesus as I walked down the street and ended up at a homeless camp called *Tent City*. As only God could orchestrate, there were a couple of Christians sleeping in tests at the homeless camp. I teamed up with them, and we started sharing the Gospel. This was a great experience and I felt like it was what I was supposed to be doing. Maybe this was my purpose.

While this was a great experience, temptation was all around me. Many in the camp were addicted to drugs and alcohol, as well as a lot of criminal activity. God had to supernaturally protect me from these temptations since this was the environment that I had been exposed to most of my life. Only God kept me sober during this time and allowed me to avoid these temptations.

At the camp, I met a guy who had just gotten out of prison and was totally intoxicated. We sat alone around a fire that night, and I shared my faith with him. Within a few moments, he freaked out, stood up, and walked toward me. I knew in my heart he was coming to hurt me, and suddenly, a voice deep inside of me yelled out,

"Shut up and sit down in the name of Jesus!" He sat back down, and I shared the Gospel with him. I immediately saw him set free. The next morning, he didn't touch a drink and then joined up with my other Christian friends and me. We started to disciple him. What an awesome experience to see someone set free, especially from something that had a hold on me, as well.

In only a couple of months of living at this homeless camp, I came away with a new lease on life and some amazing healing stories. Would this be the break I needed to turn my life around?

Taking Care of Business

Through my experience at the homeless camp, as well as spending time with God, I felt obligated to take care of some legal issues back in Ohio before I could move forward with my life. When I arrived in Ohio, I stayed at a friend's house. I locked myself in a room because I didn't want to be tempted by the pull of my addictions. I knew the only way, not to relapse, was to stay close to God.

While there, the MS symptoms became worse. At times, my motor skills stopped functioning, causing my muscles to atrophy. The only way to get back on my feet was to be admitted into a nursing home. While at the nursing home, I tried to make the most of my time there. I had fun rolling around in my wheelchair, singing, and encouraging others. I rolled around singing the song, *Jesus Loves Me* and sharing the Gospel with patients, staff, and visitors. One time, I was even asked to conduct a church service on Sunday morning all while being in a wheelchair. Looking back, it sounds unbelievable, but there was a mixture of good and evil taking place. My time in the nursing home allowed me to reflect on the times I spent in jail. When I look back, I can see there were some good times as well as a time where my life was spared.

One night after partying with friends, we went to a drug house to collect the money and drugs that were owed to us. We were desperate and determined to get what was owed to us. Our intentions were not only to collect the money and drugs but also to do harm to the dealers if they didn't give us what we wanted.

As I knocked on the door, cops answered, and of course, wanted to know why we were there. When they asked for our IDs, they discovered that I had a warrant out for my arrest along with one of my friends. I was handcuffed, and off to jail I went as well as my friend. I believe this is another example of God stepping in to protect me from myself by having the cops at this drug house at the exact time I was about to do something stupid. Since the jail was full, I had to sleep on a mat on the floor.

Another experience in jail enabled me to share Jesus with my cellmate, and he gave his life to the Lord. Even though I was a mess, God was able to use me by sharing about Jesus. So many times, I tried to run away like Jonah in the Bible, but God kept speaking to me through my thoughts. I would get angry and told Him, "I'm not serving you." Fortunately, God never left me and continued to try to help me each time I entered jail or rehab. I look back at these moments and know that they were gifts from God.

I remained at the nursing home for about two months, and the fear of relapsing and dealing with the pain and symptoms from MS were becoming overwhelming. I cried out to God, "I can't do this anymore. I can't deal with all of this anymore." I thought that if I didn't commit 100 percent to God, then when I left the nursing home, I would die.

By the time I was released from the nursing home, I was physically, but not mentally, stronger. I knew I was still in a bad way. My thoughts were scattered, and while I didn't understand or know enough about God, I knew I needed Him to carry me through this journey. While I didn't have head knowledge about God, the Bible, and Jesus, I had an intuitive knowledge of Him.

I needed to commit my heart 100 percent to Him. I'm not sure how I knew this, but I did. Back at my friend's house (where I made the decision to stay clean and sober), I started to search the internet for a Christian teacher. I told God, "I'm gonna stay clean and follow You." I also prayed and asked Him, "Lead me to a Christian teacher online to help me understand You; one that is easy for someone simple like me."

I needed someone who could help me understand the Bible. God led me directly to the perfect teacher for me. Andrew Wommack made everything easy to understand, and I was so thankful to God. I would listen to his teachings, worship, and pray all day. As I did this, the emotional healing process started. It wasn't an overnight experience for me. It took several years, but I eventually was set free from the horrible depression and thoughts of wanting to drink and killing myself that had tried to rob my mind. I was set free from the stress, guilt, condemnation, and shame that I felt was harming the people in my life.

As I mentioned, this emotional healing process didn't happen overnight, but as I began to experience the healing changes inside of me, the outward signs were visible. Once I stopped drinking and taking drugs, my physical body became stronger.

I knew I was in the fight of my life, and I was determined not to go back. If I went back to the lifestyle I had lived for so many years, I would die—now, I wanted to live. God was guiding and helping me through this process, and I was radically pursuing Him. The teacher God had led me to online was amazing and had great revelation. He taught about healing, which of course, was a topic that interested me. He spoke about emotional and physical healing, which is exactly what I needed. I listened and learned all day long and as I did this, I would go out and meet others who also needed to understand healing. This understanding helped me to pray for people who needed healing and I saw amazing healings. But what about my healing?

.

CHAPTER 7

Fighting Faith vs. Resting Faith

While attending a church picnic in Ohio, I noticed a man wearing a neck brace. I sat across from him and felt a strong desire to pray for him. I had been studying healing and understood what the Bible said about it. I asked him what happened to his neck, and he shared that he had a bone disc issue. I asked him, "Can I pray for you?" He replied, "Absolutely." I laid my hand on his neck and said, "In Jesus' name, bone disc be healed." That was it! Then I said, "Hey man, have a good day." I grabbed something to eat and left for home.

A week passed, and when I went back to church, several people approached me to let me know that the man I had prayed for went to the doctor the next day because he was feeling so good. The doctor gave him an MRI, which showed he was completely healed. This man was two days away from having surgery to repair the bone disc and now the test showed there was no need. He was completely healed. Praise Jesus! That was the first time I prayed for someone and it not only changed his life but mine as well. I knew and believed what the Word of God said, and it became real to me. I knew exactly what God wanted me to do with the rest of my life.

It became apparent that God wanted to use me to help others learn and see healings manifest in their bodies as well as my body. This healing journey became so real. It wasn't just something I was reading about in the Bible, but it was happening as I prayed for people. The healings were being confirmed by doctors. I saw the man who I prayed for in church with no neck brace. I knew God was more than just words on a page and that He now lived inside of me by the power of the Holy Spirit. In the Bible, Paul, a disciple of Jesus, said we are to become a living epistle—a witness to God's way of life.

> *Clearly you are an epistle of Christ, ministered by us, written not with ink but by the Spirit of the living God, not on tablets of stone but on tablets of flesh, that is, of the heart.*
> (2 Corinthians 3:3 NKJV)

That was what was happening to me, and these experiences were drawing me into an even deeper hunger to know God. As I got into God's Word to learn more, I saw throughout the Gospels (Matthew, Mark, Luke, and John) and the book of Acts that everyone who came to Jesus was receiving healings in their bodies. I thought, *Like, man, that's for me.* As I continued to read and study God's Word, I started to realize that it's not limited to when Jesus walked on the earth.

I saw in the Scriptures how a major part of Jesus' ministry was walking around healing the sick and doing good. As I continued to dive deeper, I read where He taught His disciples how to heal the sick, which included how to teach others to heal the sick. Jesus showed how to lay hands on the sick, and He said, "They will recover." Not maybe or sometimes, but they will recover.

> *They will take up serpents; and if they drink anything deadly, it will by no means hurt them; they will lay hands on the sick, and they will recover.*
> (Mark 16:18 NKJV)

After reading the Gospels, I read in the book of Acts how the disciples continued Jesus' ministry after he died. The disciples and other followers were performing these same healings that Jesus did while on earth. Jesus went around healing the sick and doing good. My heart leaped with excitement that God was healing people through Jesus' disciples even after He died. Jesus taught His disciples, and they, in turn, taught others and that teaching continues to be passed down and healing is for today just as it was over 2,000 years ago. After this revelation, I knew what I needed to do—go after healing!

The only way I knew to do this was to continue reading the Scriptures. I found a scripture that says, *"And do not be conformed to this world, but be transformed by the renewing of your mind, that you may prove what is that good and acceptable and perfect will of God"* (Romans 12:2 NKJV). I took this to heart and started to renew my mind by reading nothing but healing Scriptures and healing testimonies on YouTube. I watched everything I could find about healing. I looked for good Christian teachers and evangelists that were teaching the truth about healing, and I took it all in.

As I began to process all that I was learning, I stepped out just like the disciples and laid hands on the sick. This got me fired up, and I said, "God, I see it," and I pursued Him even more. However, I hadn't seen the healing of my body, yet. I laid hands on the sick and saw supernatural healings, but for some reason, my body was still sick. I couldn't understand why other people received their healing and my issues were still hanging around. I had received emotional healing, which was great, but I wasn't free of the symptoms from MS that were still lingering in my body. My mind was being transformed as I continued to press into God's Word, but my body hadn't lined up with God's Word.

Since I was on disability because of the MS, I was able to study and meditate on God's Word every day. My studying included understanding what God said about healing. I read healing books that told me God wanted me well and the Scriptures in the Bible about healing.

I ventured out to share my walk with God with others and what I was experiencing based on what I read in the Bible. I saw what God was able to do as I laid hands on the sick. The Bible Scriptures came alive, and it wasn't just head knowledge—now I saw people healed. I saw the same things that I read about in the Bible—people healed and set free from bondage.

For several years, I continued to press into God's Word and lay hands on the sick. While I saw miracles for others, nothing seemed to be coming to pass in my body. My mind and emotions were healed from all the crazy thoughts I had lived with because of the drugs and alcohol, but it felt like my body was resisting. I couldn't understand because I believed what I had seen in the Scriptures that 2,000 years ago Jesus paid for healing for the whole world by the stripes on His back. 1 Peter 2:24 (NKJV) says,

*Who Himself bore our sins in His own body on
the tree, that we, having died to sins, might live for
righteousness—by whose stripes you were healed.*

I could see this in the Scriptures, but I was struggling to understand that I was already healed. Healing wasn't flowing in my body. It felt like I was now in a struggle to believe God's Word. I saw healings for others when I prayed and laid hands on them, yet it wasn't working for me. I was fighting to maintain the healing God had provided. I've heard it referred to as "standing on the Scriptures," and when you've done all you can to stand... keep standing. I thought I was doing that by taking the Word of God and standing (believing) with my whole heart, but for some reason, it wasn't working, and I wasn't feeling the peace or entering God's rest that Hebrews 4 indicates.

*For he who has entered His rest has himself also
ceased from his works as God did from His.*
(Hebrews 4:10 NKJV)

I was fighting in my heart, fighting out of desperation, fighting for peace, and fighting for the stripes that Jesus took on His back. I was fighting to believe that healing was mine and to make sure I didn't go back to a mindset of sickness. Now, I was always in a fight mode that included reading the Scriptures and praying for the sick in order to keep and maintain my healing. I thought that I had to continue to do these things so I wouldn't lose my healing. I had heard many testimonies of people (including Christian teachers) telling me that you can lose your healing. This information kept me in fear because I didn't want to lose my healing (what I had experienced in my mind but not yet my body). I got so tired from this fear that it made my MS symptoms worse. I was now at the point of frustration.

I was doing everything the Word of God told me to do—pray for the sick, stand on the Scriptures, and fight the good fight of faith. The Bible says that hope deferred makes the heart sick, and my hope was completely deferred. Even though I saw healing all around me, I still questioned, "Why not me?" I was about to give up because my symptoms continued to get worse.

CHAPTER 8

"God, I'm Done"

Nothing I did was working for me, and I was so frustrated with everything related to healing that I decided to go to my sister's home in Washington, D.C. I had pretty much given up on healing, which left me in a defeated mental state. Because of my lack of hope, my medical symptoms got worse, and I ended up back in the hospital again.

At the hospital, I was pumped full of steroids for three days to help get me back on my feet. Once released, I felt kind of lost since I wasn't around friends or my church family. I walked around town and went into a thrift store where I engaged in a conversation with the store owners. I shared with them about Jesus, and to my surprise, they knew Him and indicated there was a church right next door.

I said, "Wow, that's awesome!" They mentioned a guy who was coming to their church to speak. It turned out to be one of the two speakers I really liked and had been watching on YouTube. I told them I would come to their church. I wanted to be around like-minded Christians and didn't want to be alone due to the symptoms I was still experiencing. The neurological part of MS caused me to feel nervous and anxious. I had hoped the church and speakers would help me learn more about healing.

I thought, *Maybe I'll hear something that will get me back on track to receive my healing.* The teaching was good, but at the same time, I was so sick and tired of everything and didn't believe anything could work for me at this point.

For some reason, I promised God I would try once more and not give up. I told Him, "I will try once more and do whatever you want me to do." I had no idea what that would be since I thought I had done everything.

At the church, I met a lady who asked me this question, "What do you think God wants to do with your life?" It was the same question that I had asked God and myself. My response was, "There is a Bible college out west, and I feel that one day I will end up attending."

I shared with her that there is a healing school at this Bible college, and I had been listening to their teachings on healing, which enabled me to fight the physical battles I was facing. She was intrigued and asked me, "How much does it cost?" I shared with her the cost and right there, she handed me the money for the full amount for the first year as well as an iPhone. Thank You Jesus! As she gave me these items, she told me, "Go!"

I stood there for a moment in shock and disbelief as all I could say was, "Thank you." Once in my car, tears streamed down my face as I thanked God. Almost immediately, the excuses came as I spoke to God— "God, how can I do this? I'm in pain, and I'm suffering. How can I drive all the way to Colorado?" I continued, "Lord, how can I go to a place where I don't know anyone?" But before I let God respond, I said, "OK, God, I will listen to You and do it."

I packed up my $700 car with everything I owned, which fit into one suitcase, and I headed west. I registered for Charis Bible college, and I was determined to try for healing one more time. I told God, "This is it. I'm only doing this one more time. I promise to try really hard, but this is it."

I enrolled full time into the college even though I was still sick. While I listened to the teachings, I felt I already knew it all and had been doing exactly what they were saying. Since I had made a promise to God that I wouldn't quit, I continued in school while believing I had done everything possible in my ability to receive my healing. Because I am not a quitter, I would fight until the end.

At college, I gave it my all. I prayed with others and got involved in the healing school. I didn't say no to anything and ended up getting burnt out by doing too much. The MS symptoms became more intense. One day while driving home from school, my body went completely numb, and I couldn't feel anything, even my thoughts were getting mixed up. Only by the power of the Holy Spirit was I able to drive my car home. I thought I was going to die, and I didn't want to go to the doctor. I just wanted to go home and die in peace. I went to bed thinking I was going to die because the symptoms were worse than ever. Death looked good to me. I said, "God, if I die tonight, I'm happy, I'm good." I didn't expect to wake up.

The next morning, I still couldn't feel anything and had all the same issues from the previous night, but I needed to get to school. I didn't understand what was happening, but I thought if I could just get to school and sit by the fireplace, even if I died, I would at least be around people I knew. God gave me supernatural strength to drive my car to school.

A friend, Elizabeth Muren, who I had met only a few months before, came to see me and said, "I'm getting the van and taking you to the hospital." She shared with me that God revealed to her the night before that I was sick and needed to be in the hospital. I thought, *Man,*

God busted me, He told on me. I felt good knowing that God didn't want me to die and sent Elizabeth to help me out.

She drove me to the hospital, where they again filled me with steroids and got me back on my feet. When I was released from the hospital, I stayed with Elizabeth and her husband for about two weeks. During this time, Elizabeth shared stories about how important God was in her life and how she talked with God. One story that stayed with me was when she was a little girl and imagined herself walking and holding God's hand. She would ask Him questions and tell Him that she loved Him. At the time she told me this story, it didn't really make any sense to me. However, at the most difficult time in my life when I had quit, given up, and asked God for help, I then remembered Elizabeth's story, and it drew me closer to Him and helped me to see what I was missing and what was causing me to struggle. This was the beginning of my personal relationship with God.

After leaving the Muren's home, another friend, Rob, took me in for about a month, and we would read healing Scriptures together. I had started to give up and really needed to hear God's Word about healing at that time. I still had a glimmer of hope and wanted to be healed. However, I was sick and tired of being sick. While at Rob's home, he would read to me, and we had a great time in the Word but, unfortunately, when I left and was at my own place, I was too exhausted to go on and I gave up. This was between my first and second year of Bible college.

I was so tired and too exhausted to continue to try to receive my healing. You see, I had tried everything in my own strength and even had others pray for me and thought I was healed but could never retain it. I quoted the healing Scriptures, but because I didn't have a relationship with God, I had nothing to stand on and never received revelation knowledge that I was truly healed. I would run from person to person asking for prayer instead of running to God, who is the Healer.

I finally said, "God, I'm done with all of this, I'm done with this healing thing. I don't care if I'm sick. I don't care that I have MS. I don't care about this school stuff. I don't care about anything. I don't care what happens. I have my friends here, and I'm just going to hang out with them." I continued with, "I quit, and whatever happens, happens. If You can do anything, please help!" Three hours later, I had this thought in my head, like, You are healed, and I said, "No, No, No, I am not doing this again."

The next morning, the same thought crossed my mind again, You are healed. Again, I thought, Oh no, I'm not doing this again, but this time I only thought it and didn't say it out loud like I did the first time. The thought about being healed kept persisting in my head. I continued to hear in my thoughts, *You are healed.* It was repeating over and over.

I finally got to the point where I said, "God, I'm not going to try to do anything, so whatever You are doing, I'm going to get out of Your way." See, I thought I was going to have to continue to fight for my healing like I had been doing for so many years, and I didn't have any fight left in me.

Suddenly, I felt the healing taking place inside of me, and by the power of the Holy Spirit, I was given the thought that *I am healed.* I don't know how all this works, but God convinced me or talked me into my healing. To the point where now I can say without a shadow of a doubt that I am healed!

I had an amazing peace surrounding me as I stopped living for God, and God started living in me through the power of the Holy Spirit.

> *I have been crucified with Christ; it is no longer*
> *I who live, but Christ lives in me; and the life which*
> *I now live in the flesh I live by faith in the Son of*
> *God, who loved me and gave Himself for me.*
> (Galatians 2:20 NKJV)

I felt the fruit of the Spirit, *"But the fruit of the Spirit is love, joy, peace, longsuffering, kindness, goodness, faithfulness, gentleness, self-control. Against such there is no law."* (Galatians 5:22–23 NKJV) inside of me and my life changed at that moment. I didn't have to fight for my life anymore. Because of all I had been through, I had a fighting type of faith and now I found a resting faith. This resting faith enabled God to heal me from the inside out. I finally understood how to enter God's rest.

The important point to understand here, especially if you are someone who has been struggling to get your healing, is to rest in what God has already done for you. I had been trying and fighting to receive healing instead of letting God's Word come alive inside of me. I had tried so hard that I didn't give God any opportunity to heal me from the inside. Once I did, it was like God's Word started to pop off the pages. His Word came alive inside of me. It was like God started to write His Words on my heart, and I became a living epistle, a witness for God, and my life changed to be like what I had read about in the Bible. And now, it was my time to minister to others and help them change their lives too. Would I find the victory I had been reading about and was searching for?

Victory

My victory over the disease and addictions that had plagued my life for many years came when I quit trying to live for God.

As I drew closer to God, He taught me while I laid in bed with the MS symptoms. As you may recall, I wasn't the best student, so trying to read books or watch messages on TV wasn't easy for me. Since I had a relationship with God, I was able to pray, worship, and talk with Him, and He revealed to me what I needed to know by bringing certain Scriptures to life. Like the Apostle Paul, after he gave his life to the Lord, he then went into the desert alone with God for three years. God revealed to him what he needed to know, and Paul would eventually write about two-thirds of the New Testament.

As God taught me, this is what He revealed to me. Through my thoughts, God showed me that I had tried to build a "house of healing" inside of me by standing only on what the Word of God said. What does this mean? I was trying to take God's Word and do what He said in my own strength. What I was missing was asking God for help and a personal relationship with Him. I had the head knowledge about healing; however, I wasn't allowing the Holy Spirit to enable the Word to come to life inside of me. I didn't give the Holy Spirit room to breathe and move inside of me, bringing the Word of God to life inside of my heart. I believed I was in charge of my healing, and that stopped the Holy Spirit from working in me. I was trying to do everything in my own strength. I read the Scriptures and then tried to do exactly what the Word said. I fought through my symptoms and never asked God for help. Once I quit and got out of the way, it enabled God to bring healing to life in my heart by the power of the Holy Spirit.

While God was revealing this to me in my thoughts, I can't say I fully understood what was happening. But I can tell you the Scriptures I had read and studied suddenly came to life inside of me. The Scriptures that were only head knowledge were now heart knowledge, meaning they became more real to me than the symptoms I had been experiencing.

At this point, the Holy Spirit became my helper on this healing journey. The Greek word for the Holy Spirit is "Paraclete," which means helper or advocate ("Paraclete" 2020). Since I wasn't relying on the Holy Spirit to help me understand God's Word, I limited the ability of God for the manifestation of my healing.

It was like a light bulb turned on inside of me, and as God showed me that I had been limiting His ability, I made this promise to Him, "I will teach others how not to limit Your healing power."

God showed me that His children are trying to work for healing versus asking Him for help. Just like me, they are trying to do it in their strength. He continued to show me that every now and then, people are receiving their healing. However, most of His children are not seeing healing come to pass in their lives because they are trying to do it in their strength. As I made this promise to God, I asked Him to help me to articulate this revelation and explain it simply so others will understand and receive.

God now teaches me every day how to let Him live through me versus me living for Him. Even though I had been baptized in the Holy Spirit years ago, I was so strong-willed and didn't feel I needed any help from anyone, including the Holy Spirit. I think many of us are so used to doing things on our own, we don't even realize we are keeping God out of our situation. Either way, I'm here to let you know that God wants to help. He wants to be your helper and equip you with the power to heal whatever you are going through.

Once I received my revelation, it was then easy to look back and see how complicated I made my healing journey. I was reading and studying the Word; however, I wasn't enabling the Holy Spirit to bring it to life for me. It is important to read and study God's Word and then ask God to help you to understand and bring it to life for you. God showed me that once I quit, gave up, and asked God for help, was He then able to bring His Word to life in my heart. I could quote the healing Scriptures and speak them out to others, yet they weren't alive in my life because I was still trying to live for God rather than God living in me. I was so tired and burnt out trying to receive my healing, and as soon as I quit trying, I found not only Him but my healing as well.

The thoughts inside my head were now about God and helping others; they were no longer about drugs, alcohol, and getting into trouble. God even brought to remembrance something my dad had told me. He pointed me to the Gospels (Matthew, Mark, Luke, and John). He said, "Stay with them and you'll be fine." He was right. As I read the Gospels and followed the life of the disciples, I became fine. I am now enjoying life and my time with God. I have given Him all my challenges and struggles, and in return, He guides and helps me every day.

I completed my second year of school and graduated with a certificate in biblical studies. Now, I have stepped out in faith with a ministry of my own. I share God's Word through videos in the hopes that I can help others get set free from whatever struggles they are facing.

My story and journey with God are not complete. I am starting to see where my new journey is taking me. I am free from drugs, alcohol, and all the bad thoughts I had lived with for so many years. The symptoms from MS are gone, and I am no longer on disability (which I had been on for more than ten years). By the stripes of Jesus, I am completely healed and whole.

God has healed and set me free from all the emotional scars that used to bring me down and caused me to spend time in hospitals due to the drugs and alcohol and the MS. Now, I get to share my testimony and the good news of Jesus Christ around the world from Kenya to India, to Norway to Australia, and even throughout the United States. I am excited to share what God can do for anyone who comes to Jesus and asks for help.

If you have not given your life to Jesus or if you are struggling and need to be set free, you can say something like this: *"God, help me; Jesus, help me and forgive me."* Then watch what God will do for you. He will restore you to wholeness.

I pray as you read my testimony and hear my story that you get to know the powerful God I serve. God set me free, and He can set you free too.

There is hope for you because John 8:36 (NKJV) says, *"Therefore if the Son makes you free, you shall be free indeed."* That is what God did for me—He set me free. God is not a respecter of persons. What He did for me, He will do for you.

God can restore the joy that has been robbed from you. He can restore you to complete wholeness as He did for me. We have a supernatural God that wants to give you supernatural power called the Holy Spirit.

Jesus died as payment for the sins of the world. No one can make it to heaven through their own good works—that's religion. We need to accept what Jesus did on the cross to pay for our sins, including healing.

If you are struggling in any area of your life, start by asking God for help and guidance. You can have victory over any issue or situation you are facing.

There is hope for you. There is so much freedom in Christ and freedom from religion. God wants to help you today. God wants you to be healed in every way. All you must do is receive Jesus and ask Him for forgiveness in your heart and start asking God for help in Jesus' name. Amen!

CHAPTER 10

Stepping Out into Ministry

As I studied God's Word, I found in the book of Mark, where Jesus gave a command to His disciples before He ascended into heaven...

And He said to them, "Go into all the world and preach the gospel to every creature. He who believes and is baptized will be saved; but he who does not believe will be condemned. And these signs will follow those who believe: In My name they will cast out demons; they will speak with new tongues; they will take up serpents; and if they drink anything deadly, it will by no means hurt them; they will lay hands on the sick, and they will recover." So then, after the Lord had spoken to them, He was received up into heaven, and sat down at the right hand of God. And they went out and preached everywhere,

the Lord working with them and confirming the
word through the accompanying signs. Amen.

(Mark 16:15–20 NKJV)

They were told to go out into the world and preach the Gospel and heal the sick. He gave them authority and taught them that signs would accompany those who believe *"they will cast out demons"* and *"lay hands on the sick and they will recover"* (verses 17–18). Healings will be the sign that confirms God's Word is true. He also directed them to give freely because they freely received the teachings of the Lord Jesus Christ.

As a believer, I am one of His disciples, so this command applies to me as well as all believers. I accept this command and look for opportunities to share with others by going out into the streets, shopping malls, and most recently, to Kenya, Africa.

During a mission's trip to Kenya, this Scripture came to life for me as we saw amazing healing testimonies. Local pastors and I went throughout the village sharing the Gospel and praying for the locals. We went from hut to hut, and along the way, we met a woman who was asking for prayer. She was very kind and invited us into her home. As we talked, she mentioned that she had trouble with her vision. She said, "See those mountains, they are blurry to me." I asked, "Can we pray with you?"

She agreed. In Jesus' name, I commanded her eyes to open. I asked her, "What do you see?" She said, "The mountains are still blurry."

I then told her about the Scripture in Mark 8:22–25. And that we could pray again. we can pray again. Jesus prayed for a blind man and the blind man said he saw men that looked like trees. The man saw people, but they looked blurry, so Jesus put His hands on the man again and prayed. If Jesus can pray for someone twice, we can do the same. We should pray until the situation changes.

We knew that God wanted this woman healed and freed from the bondage of being blind. She didn't have running water or even electricity. We prayed again and her eyes were opened. Praise Jesus! It was not only life-changing for her but also for the pastors and me. I had never seen blind eyes open, but I knew God's Word was true and prayed with that expectation.

We continued throughout the village praying and laying hands on the sick. Two additional people received healing from deaf ears. God's miracle touch was present in that village.

At the airport on my way home, I met a group of Muslims. I clearly heard God say, "Tell them about Me." My initial thought was, *How do I break the ice?* So, I asked them, "Tell me about your god."

After hearing them talk about their god, I shared Jesus. When I grabbed one of the men's hands, the power of the Holy Spirit came all over him, and he started to weep. That is the power and demonstration of when you preach or talk about God's Word.

> *And my speech and my preaching were not with persuasive words of human wisdom, but in demonstration of the Spirit and of power.*
> (1 Corinthians 2:4 NKJV)

This man met God and saw that Jesus is real. I believe he was set free that day and that God is continuing to do a work in his life. I was obedient to hear God ask me to share Jesus with this group of men. The Quran does speak about Jesus but not as the Son of God. Also, the Quran teaches them to follow the scripture. Even their Quran points them to the Bible, but for some reason, they have overlooked this and followed after strange teaching.

God wants you healed and set free, too. What He did for those in Kenya, He will do for you, as well. If you need healing, find the healing Scriptures in the Bible, read them, meditate on them, believe, and ask God for help!

We don't need to all run off to Africa to pray and see God's miracles. We can do it anytime and anywhere, and especially in our daily routines.

Recently I was summoned for jury duty. My initial thought was, *How do I get out of this?* Over my lifetime, I had seen enough jails and courtrooms and had no desire to see one again. Because of the summons, I had to attend. Since each potential juror is questioned, I thought I would take the opportunity to share my testimony. That had to be good enough to get me thrown off the case. After they questioned everyone, they dismissed everyone except me and five others. Once the initial shocked wore off, I wondered how they could keep me as a juror, especially with my history?

The other jurors were now questioning me about my testimony and wondering how I was still functioning and didn't even look at all like the person I described. The time I spent with the jurors and during the trial was awesome. It gave me an amazing time to share about Jesus and my journey about how God set me free. We were also able to listen to the testimony of the man on trial and see an innocent man be set free from a wrong charge against him.

Here I was trying to get out of jury duty, but God was able to use it as an opportunity to share the Gospel and speak about Jesus in a courthouse. No one rejected what

I had to say and welcomed hearing my testimony. I was glad to be a part of the whole experience.

I am finding out that we all have a story to tell. We don't have to be a preacher in a church to share about Jesus and what He did for each of us. It is about sharing what Jesus did in my life and then listening and helping others to know Him.

You can use your personal testimony as an ice breaker when you meet new people as I did at the courthouse. Simply share what Jesus did for you. It doesn't have to be as crazy as my life story; maybe Jesus set you free from anger issues or the fear of flying.

And they overcame him by the blood of the Lamb
and by the word of their testimony, and they did not
love their lives to the death.
(Revelation 12:11 NKJV)

Don't be afraid to share what Jesus has done in your life. Jesus commanded us to go out into the world, but we also have opportunities every day in our daily routines. Go out into the shopping malls, or it could be while you are standing in line for coffee or a donut.

Our world is now at our fingertips; now we have the ability to reach almost anyone through social media. I have recently branched out into the internet through

Facebook, Twitter, Instagram, YouTube, and my personal web site.

I am now taking what I've learned through my experiences and making video teachings sharing how easy it is to be healed and live set free from addictions and bondages.

I believe through these teachings, you will see how much God loves you and that He truly didn't make the Christian life hard.

Then sit back and watch what God will do.

CHAPTER 11

How to Ask God for Help

Just ask! Talking with God is like talking with your wife/husband or your best friend. God wants to have a relationship with us; that is why He created us. There are so many stories in the Bible where God spoke with His people. In the Garden of Eden, God walked and talked with Adam and Eve. He spoke with Abraham. At Mt. Sinai, He spoke with Moses. God wants the same with us. He wants a relationship. He wants us to be free to talk to Him about life, our cares and concerns. He also wants to be able to talk to you. You might be thinking, *How does God talk to me?* The Bible says, in "...*a still small voice*" (1 Kings 19:11–12 NKJV).

God also speaks to us through another person. Did you ever have a question or thought, and it was answered by a friend or even someone you didn't know? It might even be through an advertisement on TV.

A relationship with God is not about church or religion. It is about talking directly to God and asking Him for help or sharing what is on your heart. Once you start talking with Him, read His Word, and spend time with Him. You'll see your relationship with Him and your Christian life take on a whole new experience.

My Christian life started to explode when the teachings I had been studying got mixed with the Holy Spirit and became more than teachings—it became real and powerful. My emotions, physical body, and even my ministry seemed to change. I thought my Christian life had already exploded when I gave my life to the Lord and was walking out what the Scriptures said. I thought that was walking the Christian life. However, after laying down my life—my whole life—did I finally understand what it meant to walk with Jesus and have a personal relationship with the Lord. I've heard the phrase having a "childlike faith" or "childlike dependency," but I never really understood or experienced it. Once I quit trying to live for God and gave Him my whole life, did I truly experience having a childlike dependence upon Him. Just as a child needs to ask their parents for help in all aspects of their lives, that is the same way we need to come to our Father. We should wake up each day and say, "Father God, I need your help in everything I do today." As we continue in our day, and something new appears, we should say, "Father God, help me." If you are fixing a car, "God, help me fix this car." If you are studying for a test, "God, help me study and retain the information I am studying." There is nothing too big or too small for us to ask God for His help. Remember, He gave us The Helper (The Holy Spirit) as our advocate and to help us with every aspect of our lives but the helper, the Holy Spirit, doesn't completely activate until we ask God for help.

We have an example in the Bible to show us how to walk and talk with God. In Genesis, Adam and Eve were in the garden, and it says they walked and talked with God. *"And they heard the sound of the LORD God walking in the garden in the cool of the day, and Adam and his wife hid themselves from the presence of the LORD God among the trees of the garden"* (Genesis 3:8 NKJV). Even before there were Scriptures or a Bible, there was just Adam, Eve, and God. God created them for relationship. That is what He wants for us. God wants us to get back to our first love

> *I know your works, your labor, your patience,*
> *and that you cannot bear those who are evil. And*
> *you have tested those who say they are apostles and*
> *are not, and have found them liars; and you have*
> *persevered and have patience, and have labored for*

My name's sake and have not become weary. Nevertheless I have this against you, that you have left your first love. Remember therefore from where you have fallen; repent and do the first works, or else I will come to you quickly and remove your lampstand from its place—unless you repent.

(Revelation 2:2–5 NKJV)

God is our first love. This scripture in the book of Revelation is very important to understand what God is saying to us. God wants a relationship with us.

What God is trying to show us is that Christians were living awesome lives, becoming great ministers of the Gospel, but He had one thing against them. They had left their first love, and this is exactly where I was in my Christian walk. I didn't have my first love (God) and that is why the Word of God wasn't working for me.

I want to stress that this is my testimony, my story, and walk with God. I share this in the hopes it may help someone else who might be able to relate to my story. I pray you might be able to get something from my story and not reject it just because it isn't applicable to your walk. Each one of our walks is different.

I am not an expert, and all I can share is my experiences and what God has shown me in the Scriptures. In the book of Revelation, God showed me that He was looking to live inside of me and wanted me to come back to Him. See, just like in Revelation 2:2–5, I was living for God and doing a lot of great works, especially after I was born-again and had a personal encounter with Him. However, I wasn't walking with Him and asking Him for help. I wasn't walking like Adam and Eve did in the Garden.

I'm learning how to walk with God and not fall back into works by working for God. The only way I know how to do this is, "God help me." This enables me to let God live through me...

> *I have been crucified with Christ; it is no longer*
> *I who live, but Christ lives in me; and the life which*
> *I now live in the flesh I live by faith in the Son of*
> *God, who loved me and gave Himself for me.*
> (Galatians 2:20 NKJV)

...and that only comes through my relationship with Him and walking and talking with Him each day. Here are some Scriptures that might help you learn how to get God to live through you versus you trying to live for God.

Ephesians 3 is a powerful book that you might want to spend some time reading and meditating on. I'd like to point out Ephesians 3:17–19 talks about how to know the love of Christ, which passes knowledge that you may be filled with all the fullness of God.

> *That Christ may dwell in your hearts through faith; that you, being rooted and grounded in love, may be able to comprehend with all the saints what is the width and length and depth and height—to know the love of Christ which passes knowledge; that you may be filled with all the fullness of God."*
>
> (Ephesians 3:17–19 NKJV)

Here is my interpretation of what this Scripture means, and how it's working for me. The word "know" here means a personal, intimate understanding. Passes knowledge means beyond our natural thinking. Putting this all together, I believe it is walking and talking with God daily and asking Him for help and having a childlike dependence on Him. Here is how a conversation with God may go each day. "God, I need Your help." "God, help me write this paper for school." "God, help me get my work done in time for my meeting." "God, would You like to go shopping with me?"

You should be able to have a dialogue with God, talking back and forth with Him. When you have a personal relationship with God, you should be able to hear His voice. God speaks to each of us differently. It is important to hear God's voice and be able to recognize it. The Bible says, *"My sheep hear My voice, and I know them, and they follow Me"* (John 10:27 NKJV). When we know (have that intimate knowledge) God, we know His voice vs. hearing our thoughts or that of someone else.

Having a conversation with God and asking Him for help was a major piece I was missing. While I was learning Scriptures about God, I never heard anyone tell me about a personal, intimate relationship with Him. I knew how to do the Scriptures; however, I didn't know how to talk with God or have an interaction with Him. I surely didn't know that God could speak to me in my thoughts.

I threw myself into the Scriptures and tried to stand on them, speak them, maintain them, and even receive them. I tried to do everything people were telling me to do to obtain my healing. I could even quote all the healing Scriptures. While knowing God's Word is important, one main point is also to know God and His love. We need to be filled with the fullness of His love. The only way I know how to do this is by spending one-on-one time with God, asking Him for His help and reading the Scriptures.

God showed me that He didn't make healing hard. If we have a loving Father, why would He make healing hard? It became me making it hard by trying to receive it out of my strength. This was because I wasn't walking and talking with God, and I wasn't asking Him for help. I spent my time just reading the Word and trying to do exactly what it said. I did not understand what the Word was saying about this relationship with Him about how Jesus went to the mountains to talk with God. For me, there was so much that I was missing by just doing and missing the point that God wants a personal relationship with me.

The manifestation of my healing from MS wasn't happening since I couldn't see or understand the love of God. Once I quit trying to live for Him, asked Him for help, and started talking with Him, that is when the Word of God became alive, leaped off the pages and into my heart, and the fruit of the Spirit started flowing through me.

Now, God is working out everything in my life, and things are becoming easier because I am doing it with Him. *"For My yoke is easy and My burden is light"* (Matthew 11:30 NKJV). God is showing us our walk with Him should be easy, and if we believe what the Bible says that God loves us, then we know He wouldn't make healing hard or keep it from us.

We make healing hard when we try to live for God or feel we need to complete a twelve-step program to receive our healing. Many times, people want the exact steps they need to do in order to get their healing, when God is saying, "Just have a relationship with Me. Rest in Me, ask Me for help, and I will bring the right healing Scripture to life inside of you."

If you are struggling with healing or anything, I want you to know that God loves you and He wants the best for you. 1 John 4 shows us how to know God through love. God is love, He loves you, and is pouring out His love into your heart by the power of the Holy Spirit. In Romans 5:5 (NKJV), it says,

> *Now hope does not disappoint, because the love of God has been poured out in our hearts by the Holy Spirit who was given to us.*

God is pouring His love out to you. However, if you are trying to live for God and doing it in your strength, you limit or block the ability to receive God's love and His healing power. God is not withholding healing or the fruit of the Spirit from you; it is you trying to live for God vs. God living through you.

As this relationship develops, you will then trust His Word, and can fully understand that *by His stripes you are healed* (Isaiah 53:5). Because He spoke that Word to you and you are no longer trying to get it, stand on it, or fight to receive it. You will know without a shadow of a doubt that it is yours and that Jesus died for you to walk in total healing and wholeness.

Conclusion

Only through God's grace and love could a mischievous boy, a drug and alcohol addicted young man turn his life completely around not only to change his life but help change the lives of others.

God's grace is defined as unmerited favor, which means it is a gift that is freely given by God for us to either accept or reject this gift. Ephesian 2:8–9 (NKJV) says,

> *For by grace you have been saved through faith,*
> *and that not of yourselves; it is the gift of God, not of*
> *works lest anyone should boast.*

Grace is what God does because He loves each of us so much that He gave us His only Son. His Son took our sins and our sicknesses.

For God so loved the world that He gave His only begotten Son, that whoever believes in Him should not perish but have everlasting life.

(John 3:16 NKJV)

This is very different from religion, which is what we do for God. Religion teaches us we must be good enough to earn salvation, to earn God's love, and to live by all the commandments. I tried religion and thought I had to do something to get God to heal me. Through my journey, I learned that God had already provided all I needed by His grace through my faith in Jesus Christ. By grace, He has provided, righteousness, healing, prosperity, and victory. Our part is to believe through faith in Jesus' death and His resurrection and then receive this grace gift by faith.

I also learned that God's love was not based on my performance. How could it be when I was doing everything wrong, and at times, illegally. How could a just God love me when I felt unlovable? How could a loving God look at me and see there was anything good inside of me? How could a righteous God see me and call me righteous? *It is because He is Love.*

God's very nature and character is love. Everything God does is based on His love for us and not based on anything we could ever do to be accepted. Understanding God's love for me was one of the most important revelations I could have ever experienced. God loved me when I was doing drugs, getting arrested, and struggling with health issues. He loved me despite my situation and circumstances. When I realized there wasn't anything I could do to earn His love, it set me free. There is freedom in God's love.

When I fell in love with God, it was easy to say no to the temptations and my additions. In Matthew 4, Jesus was tempted by the devil and overcame those temptations because He knew He was the "beloved Son" of God. Jesus knew His value to His Father.

We need this same understanding and knowledge. In Hosea 4:6 (NKJV), it says,

> *My people are destroyed (perish) for lack of knowledge.*

We need to see ourselves as to how God sees us. Genesis 1:27 (NKJV) says,

> *So God created man in His own image; in the image of God He created him; male and female He created them.*

The next verse says, *"Then God blessed them..."* These verses show us that we are made in the image of God. As born-again believers, we have the same DNA as Jesus. DNA carries our genetic information and stores our distinctive characteristics and qualities. When we accepted Jesus as our Lord and Savior, God breathed into our spirit the same characteristics and qualities of Jesus. Wow, now that is awesome!

I know many don't feel like this is possible because they may still have negative thoughts or feelings, but you don't have to accept those thoughts or feelings. God tells us to renew our minds to what He says about us. God calls us His Beloved just as He called Jesus, His Beloved! The word "beloved" means dearly loved, someone who is greatly loved ("Beloved" 2020). The Old Testament, Song of Solomon, gives us a picture of this word, "beloved," as it describes the deep affection newlyweds have for each other.

To better understand this type of love, we can look to our Heavenly Father and Jesus as examples. In 1 John 4:8, 16, we learn that God is love, and in verse 19, we see that God first loved us. The Gospel of John and 1, 2, and 3 John's writings are all about love. God doesn't need us to love Him, but He delights and takes pleasure in our love toward Him (Psalm 147:11). The Creator of the universe who gave us life, breathe, and every spiritual blessing (Ephesians 1:3) wants to have a personal relationship with us and desires our love in return.

God loved us so much that He came to earth to save us from eternal separation from Him (John 3:16). What is even more amazing is that He tied healing to forgiveness! When God forgave us for our sins and saved us, healing was included in the package. This gift of love from God is so awesome and powerful that He wants us to live a healed and whole type of life—free from sickness, poverty, oppression, depression, pain, etc.

1 Peter 2:24 (NKJV) shows us that healing is part of Christ's atonement. Peter is talking about Jesus in this verse:

Who Himself bore our sins in His own body on the tree, that we, having died to sins, might live for righteousness—by whose stripes you were healed.

John 3:16 shows us that God so loved the world (everyone), that He sent Jesus to die on the cross so we could live an everlasting life that includes healing, wholeness, and abundant life.

John, a disciple of Jesus, reveals in the Gospel of John that he is the disciple that Jesus loved. We might think this is arrogant on his part, but I think we should all strive to be able to say the same, "I am the one that Jesus loves." John walked with Jesus on an intimate basis and had the confidence to say that Jesus loved him. This intimate, personal type of love is available to each one of us. A love that is so powerful and caring that healing flows out from Him. We are all children of God; we are sons and daughters, and someone God loves so much that He physically came to earth to reveal and give us all His blessings.

If you are a prodigal son or daughter and feel that your sins, your crazy way of living, or the things you've done can't be forgiven, I'm here to tell you that God only sees your righteousness and anything you've done in your past stays in the past. Like the saying, "What happens in Vegas, stays in Vegas" —As believers, our past, present, and future have all been forgiven by what Jesus did on the cross.

I am living proof that God can forgive what we've done in the past. I am someone God gave grace and love to even during those challenging and troubled times. God is love, and He wants you to live healed, whole, and set free.

Don't reject the free gift that God has provided through His grace. Come to Him and be set free!

Appendix

Knowing and speaking God's Word is critical during any challenging situation. Here are some Scriptures that helped me through my hard times. Ask God to give you revelation knowledge about these Scriptures, and they will come to life in your heart. All Scriptures are from the New King James Version of the Bible.

John 3:16–17

For God so loved the world that He gave His only begotten Son, that whoever believes in Him should not perish but have everlasting life. For God did not send His Son into the world to condemn the world, but that the world through Him might be saved.

Psalm 107:20

He sent His word and healed them, And delivered them from their destructions.

Romans 4:20

He did not waver at the promise of God through unbelief, but was strengthened in faith, giving glory to God.

Romans 5:5

Now hope does not disappoint, because the love of God has been poured out in our hearts by the Holy Spirit who was given to us.

Romans 8:1

There is therefore now no condemnation to those who are in Christ Jesus, who do not walk according to the flesh, but according to the Spirit.

Romans 8:28

And we know that all things work together for good to those who love God, to those who are the called according to His purpose.

Romans 10:17

So then faith comes by hearing, and hearing by the word of God.

Romans 12:2

And do not be conformed to this world, but be transformed by the renewing of your mind, that you may prove what is that good and acceptable and perfect will of God

Romans 15:4

For whatever things were written before were written for our learning, that we through the patience and comfort of the Scriptures might have hope.

Romans 15:13

Now may the God of hope fill you with all joy and peace in believing, that you may abound in hope by the power of the Holy Spirit.

1 Corinthians 2: 9–10

But as it is written: "Eye has not seen, nor ear heard, Nor have entered into the heart of man The things which God has prepared for those who love Him." But God has revealed them to us through His Spirit. For the Spirit searches all things, yes, the deep things of God.

Ephesians 2:8

For by grace you have been saved through faith, and that not of yourselves; it is the gift of God.

Ephesians 3:17–19

That Christ may dwell in your hearts through faith; that you, being rooted and grounded in love, may be able to comprehend with all the saints what is the width and length and depth and height—to know the love of Christ which passes knowledge; that you may be filled with all the fullness of God.

...This is relationship with God.

1 Peter 2:24

Who Himself bore our sins in His own body on the tree, that we, having died to sins, might live for righteousness—by whose stripes you were healed.

1 John 4:18

There is no fear in love; but perfect love casts out fear, because fear involves torment. But he who fears has not been made perfect in love.

References

"Beloved." 2020. Definitions.Net, STANDS4 LLC. 2020. https://www.definitions.net/definition/beloved.

"Multiple Sclerosis: What Is MS? Overview, Risk Factors and Outlook." 2019. WebMD LLC. 2019. https://www.webmd.com/multiple-sclerosis/what-is-multiple-sclerosis#1.

"Paraclete." 2020. Bible Study Tools. 2020. https://www.biblestudytools.com/dictionary/paraclete/.

The Holy Bible: The New King James Version [NKJV]. 1999, Nashville: Thomas Nelson. https://www.biblegateway.com/versions/New-King-James-Version-NKJV-Bible/#booklist

About the Author

Jeremiah Klaas enjoyed getting into trouble. His childhood and teenage years were characterized by inner turmoil. He was asked to leave high school, which drove him toward even more trouble and suicidal thoughts. Drugs and alcohol masked the pain during these years; however, this increased the emptiness that lived inside of him. His life spiraled out of control for many years until he allowed God to fill the void.

Jeremiah's heart is to share his amazing testimony of the power of Jesus and how God can take someone whose life was completely broken and turn it around to find true victory in Christ.

Jeremiah Klass Ministry is a teaching ministry established to see others set free through the power of the simplicity of the Gospel. Free from the bondage of religion and the deceptions this world is offering and replace it with unconditional love and grace only found through a personal relationship with the Lord Jesus Christ.

To stay in touch with Jeremiah or contact him, please visit his web site at *www.jeremiahklaas.com*